King James about W
in the Chu
and in the Bible.

This Book was created primarily
to encourage and inspire
in building an intimate Moment
with God.

It covers a wide Variety
of Situations in Life
and can support you
in your Hour of Need.

Each verse
has its own Prayer
written by Annalien Lenk
and inspired by the Holy Spirit.

Page Setting and Design
by Kurt Lenk.

Proverbs 31:30 KJV

Favour is deceitful, and beauty is vain:

but a woman that feareth the Lord, she shall be praised.

Prayer by Millie Smith

Father in heaven,
   I thank you for all
      that you have done for me
     and I know
        where my help comes from.

I don't have much to give in return,
so here is my heart Lord
   and I pray that my heart would be
   a reflection of yours.

     Teach me to be more
     like you and help me
      to become the women
        you have made me to be.

I surrender all things to you
    and pray
    that you guard my heart O Lord,
      in your precious name I pray.

        Amen

Titus 2:3-5 KJV

The aged women likewise,
that they be in behaviour
as becometh holiness,

not false accusers,
not given to much wine,
teachers of good things;

That they may teach
the young women to be sober,
to love their husbands,
to love their children,

To be discreet, chaste,
keepers at home, good,
obedient to their own husbands,
that the word of God
be not blasphemed.

Prayer by Millie Smith

My Lord, I come here before you,
    to ask that you grant me wisdom
        and understanding in your ways.
Teach me to be slow to anger,
    to be patient with your timing and others.
Lord create in me a clean heart
    and a sober mind so that I can be more like you.
Let my words be your words,
    so I can speak life and not death
        to honour your name.
    Teach me to love my husband
        and children, as you love the church ..
        to keep me from the gossip
            and rumours that surround me,
    so that I may not be tempted
        by the ways of the world.
Most of all, my father
    let me pass on this wisdom
        you have given to me,
        to the woman that surround me
    and the generations to come.

    In the name of Jesus, I pray

    Amen

Psalm 46:5 KJV

God is in the midst of her; she shall not be moved: God shall help her, and that right early.

Prayer by Millie Smith

My father in heaven,
you are my salvation
and my strength..

Let your holy spirit lead me
and direct my path.

My father,
keep me in the shadow of your wings
and protect me
from any harm
that comes my way.

Lord, you are my strong fortress
and I will not be shaken.

In Jesus name I pray.

Amen

Proverbs 31:29 KJV

Many daughters have done virtuously, but thou excellest them all.

Prayer by Millie Smith

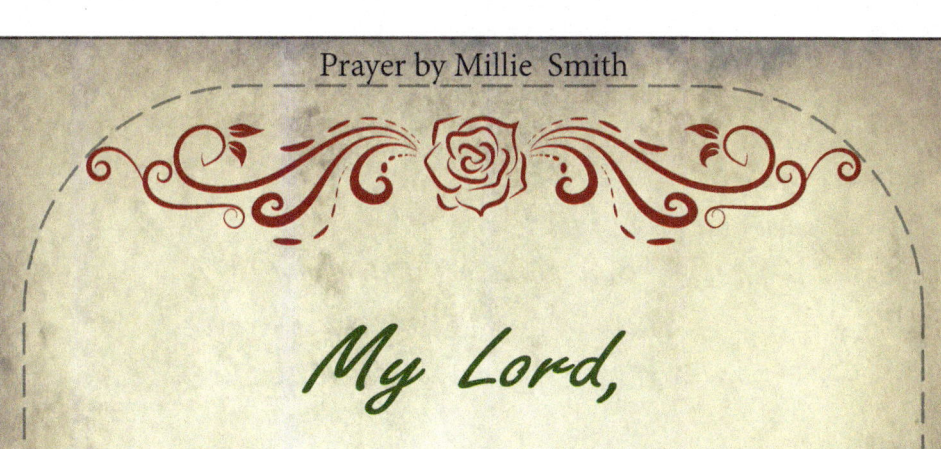

My Lord,

*please teach me
how to be—
and carry myself
as a virtuous woman.*

*In the name of Jesus
I pray.*

Amen

1 Peter 3:1-7 KJV

Likewise, ye wives, be in subjection
    to your own husbands;
        that, if any obey not the word,
            they also may without the word
        be won by the conversation of the wives;

While they behold your chaste conversation
    coupled with fear.
        Whose adorning let it not be
        that outward adorning
        of plaiting the hair,
          and of wearing of gold,
        or of putting on of apparel;

        But let it be the hidden man of the heart,
          in that which is not corruptible,
          even the ornament of a meek
          and quiet spirit, which is
        in the sight of God of great price.

        For after this manner
in the old time the holy women also,
who trusted in God, adorned themselves,
being in subjection unto their own husbands:

        Even as Sara obeyed Abraham,
          calling him lord: whose daughters ye are,
          as long as ye do well,
          and are not afraid with any amazement…

Prayer by Annalien Lenk

Oh my Holy Lord and Father,
may I always be a shining light
and comforter
to my own husband,
just like You are for me.

May my lips always proclaim
your goodness and mercy.

Let me be the women
that You made me to be.

LOVING, KIND
AND CARING.

AMEN.

Ephesians 5:22 KJV

*Wives,
submit yourselves
unto your own husbands,
as unto the Lord.*

Prayer by Annalien Lenk

Lord my God
I promise to always submit
to my own husband.

Please help and guide me
to always be the best wife
and mother to my family.

Give me strength
every day
to be better
than the day before.

I ask this
in the Mighty Name of Jesus.

AMEN

Proverbs 6:20 KJV

*My son,

keep thy father's commandment

and forsake not

the law of thy mother.*

Prayer by Annalien Lenk

Dear Father in Heaven,

please help me to always obey your commandments as it is written.

Help me to never forsake your Holy Law.

You are — and you will always be the reason I live.

In The Mighty Name of Jesus.

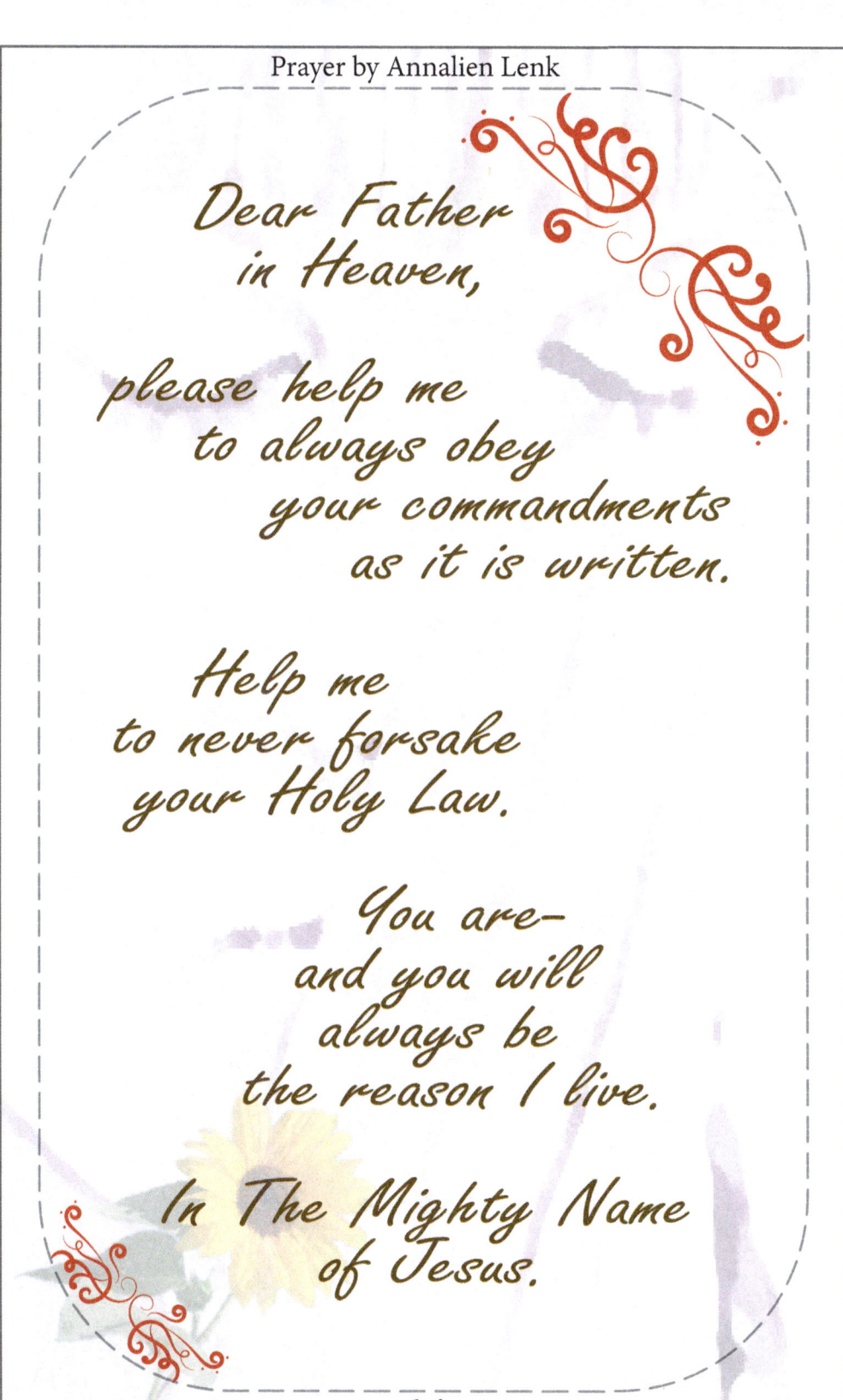

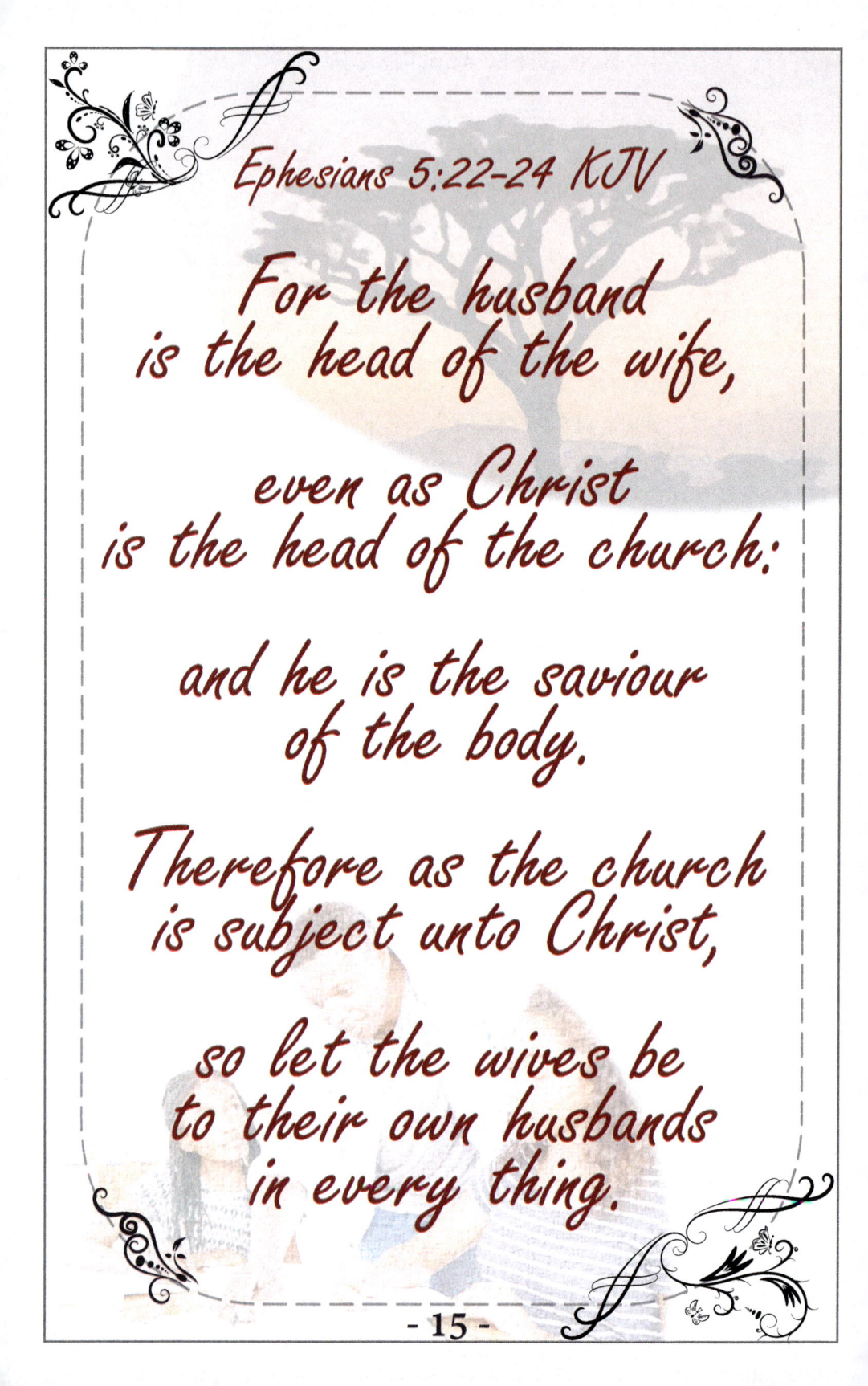

Ephesians 5:22-24 KJV

For the husband is the head of the wife,

even as Christ is the head of the church:

and he is the saviour of the body.

Therefore as the church is subject unto Christ,

so let the wives be to their own husbands in every thing.

Prayer by Millie Smith

Father God,

*I pray that you shall remain
in the centre of our relationship
and that we will put you first always.*

*Let us love one another
as you love the church
and let us keep praying
for strength, healing, joy,
and patience for one another.*

*In the name of Jesus Christ
I pray.*

Amen

Proverbs 31:25 KJV

Strength and honour are her clothing; and she shall rejoice in time to come.

Prayer by Millie Smith

Lord, Let your daughters
put on the full armour of God

and be clothed in righteousness,
ready to face any battle..

..because we know
that joy will come in the morning.

In Jesus name.

Amen

1 Corinthians 14:34 KJV

Let your women keep silence in the churches:

for it is not permitted unto them to speak;

but they are commanded to be under obedience as also saith the law.

Prayer by Annalien Lenk

Lord I pray

to be obedient to Your law
as a Women of God.

I humble myself
to You and my own husband.

I will obey
and keep Your word.

In the Name of The Father,
the Son and The Holy Spirit I pray.

Amen

Luke 10:38-42 KJV

Now it came to pass, as they went, that he entered into a certain village:

and a certain woman named Martha received him into her house.

And she had a sister called Mary, which also sat at Jesus' feet, and heard His word.

But Martha was cumbered about much serving, and came to him, and said,

Lord, dost thou not care that my sister hath left me to serve alone? Bid her therefore that she help me.

And Jesus answered and said unto her, Martha, Martha, thou art careful and troubled about many things:

But one thing is needful: and Mary hath chosen that good part, which shall not be taken away from her.

Prayer by Annalien Lenk

Almighty God

my Father in Heaven,
today I pray to always be humble
and understanding to Your ways, Lord.

Lead- and guide me today,
so that I will always know
that You are with me
and that I may find love
and peace – at Your feet my God.

AMEN

Titus 2:3 KJV

The aged women likewise,
that they be in behaviour
as becometh holiness,
not false accusers,
not given to much wine,
teachers of good things;

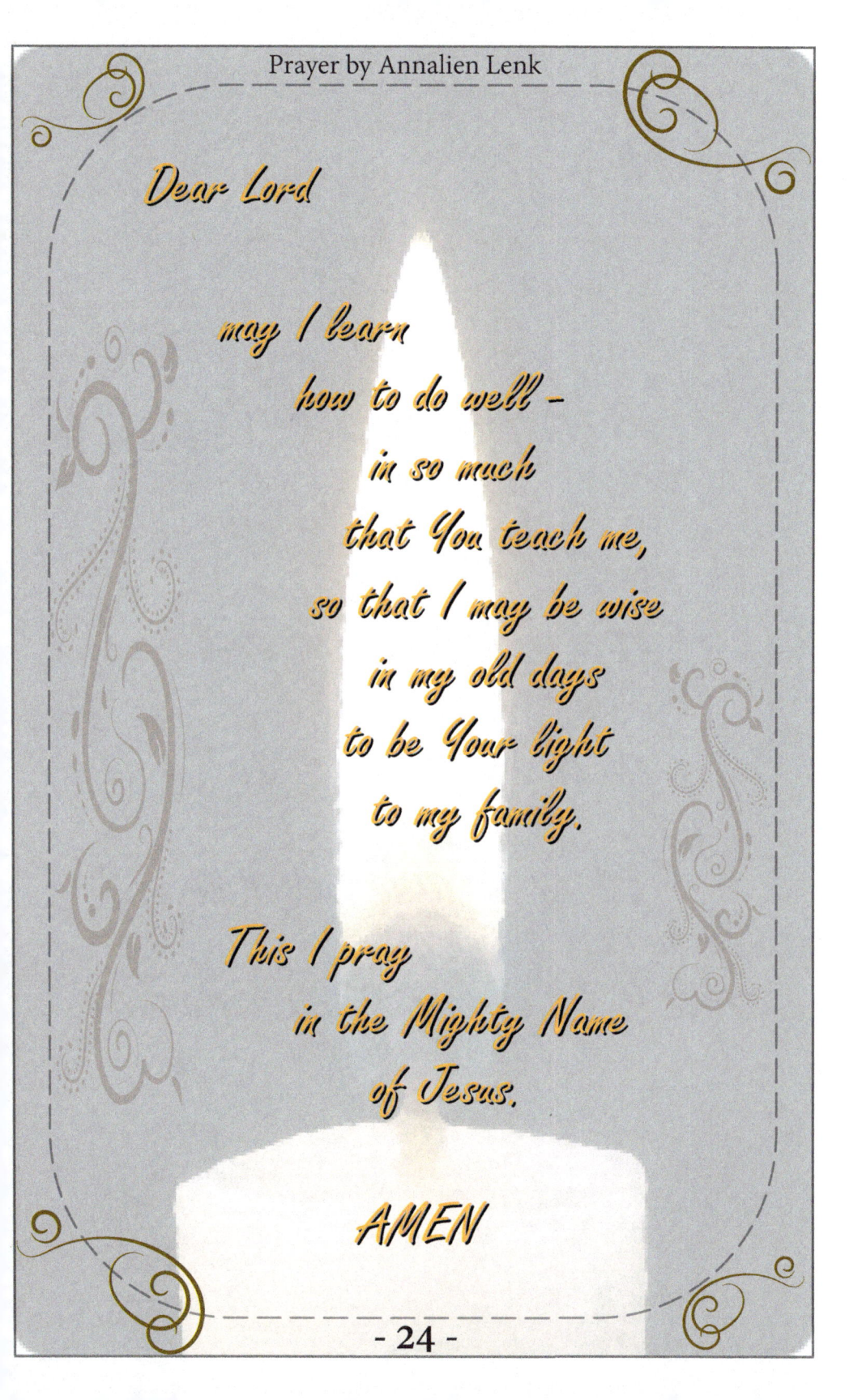

Prayer by Annalien Lenk

Dear Lord

may I learn
how to do well –
in so much
that You teach me,
so that I may be wise
in my old days
to be Your light
to my family.

This I pray
in the Mighty Name
of Jesus.

AMEN

Proverbs 11:22 KJV

As a jewel of gold in a swine's snout, so is a fair woman which is without discretion.

Prayer by Annalien Lenk

My God,

I do not care
how the world perceives me
and what they think of me.

The only thing I care for
is what You think of me, Lord
and that my name is written
in the book of life,
so I can dwell
in your house Lord, forever.

AMEN

1 Timothy 5:1-2 KJV

*Rebuke not an elder,
but intreat him as a father;
and the younger men as brethren;*

*The elder women as mothers;
the younger as sisters, with all purity.*

Prayer by Annalien Lenk

Father in heaven,

   you have created
      all man equally.

May we have patience
   and love for each other today.

That we can have eternal life.

AMEN

Isaiah 3:12 KJV

*As for my people,
children are their oppressors,
and women rule over them.*

*O my people,
they which lead thee
cause thee to err,
and destroy the way
of thy paths.*

Prayer by Annalien Lenk

My prayer today
is of grace for my children, Lord.

That they will
always honour their parents
and that we always guide them
in the right way

In Your Name we pray.

AMEN

Matthew 27:55-56 KJV

And many women were there beholding afar off, which followed Jesus from Galilee, ministering unto him:

Among which was Mary Magdalene, and Mary the mother of James and Joses, and the mother of Zebedees children.

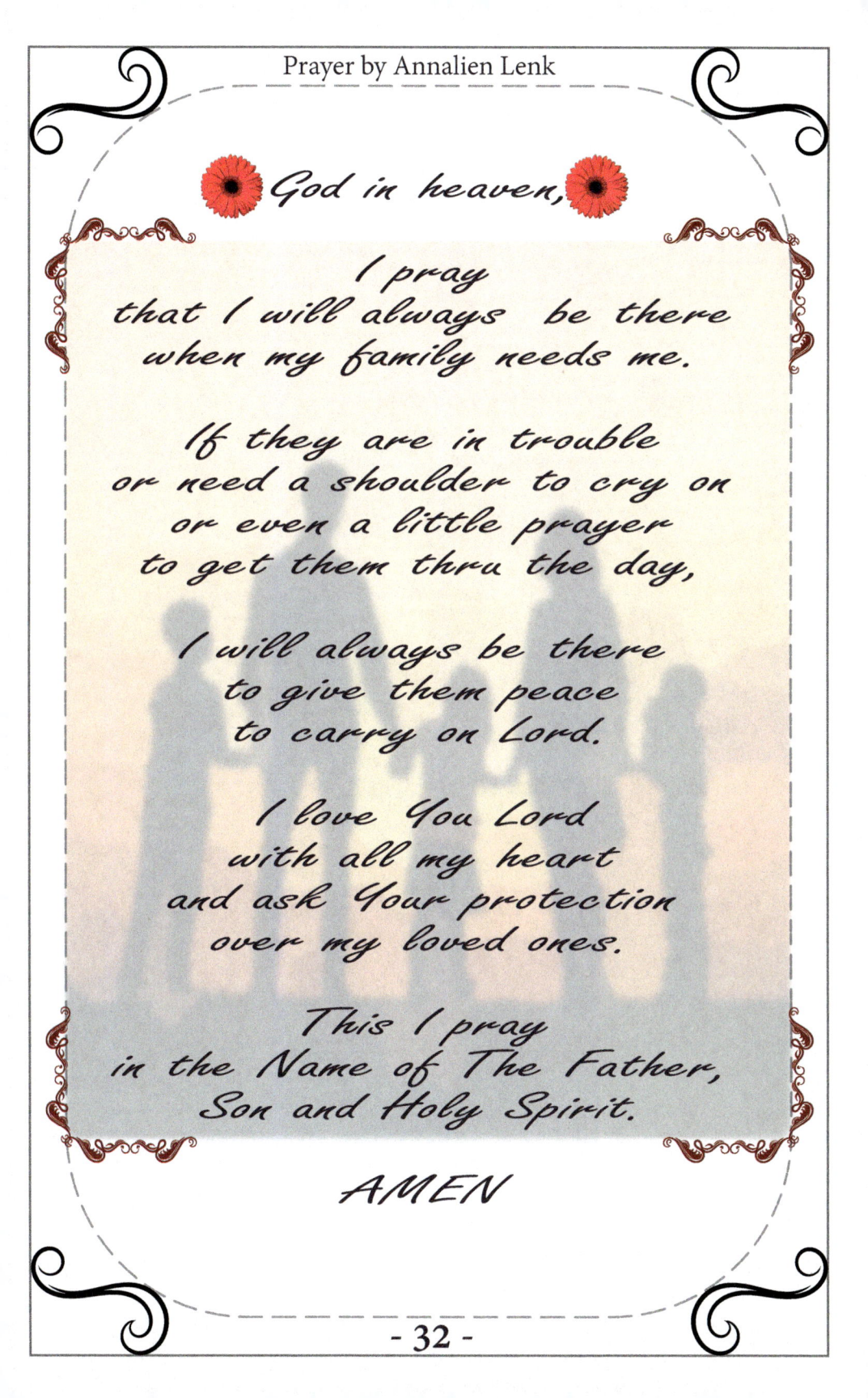

Prayer by Annalien Lenk

God in heaven,

I pray
that I will always be there
when my family needs me.

If they are in trouble
or need a shoulder to cry on
or even a little prayer
to get them thru the day,

I will always be there
to give them peace
to carry on Lord.

I love You Lord
with all my heart
and ask Your protection
over my loved ones.

This I pray
in the Name of The Father,
Son and Holy Spirit.

AMEN

1 Timothy 2:11-14 KJV

Let the woman learn
    in silence
        with all subjection.

But I suffer not a woman to teach,
nor to usurp authority over the man,
    but to be in silence.

    For Adam was first formed, then Eve.

And Adam was not deceived,
    but the woman being deceived
        was in the transgression.

Prayer by Annalien Lenk

Lord,

you are my strength,
my salvation and my defence.

You are my Father,
my voice and my God Forever.

I will always obey Your word
in the Holy of Holies.

In Your mighty Name.

AMEN

Song of Solomon 4:1 KJV

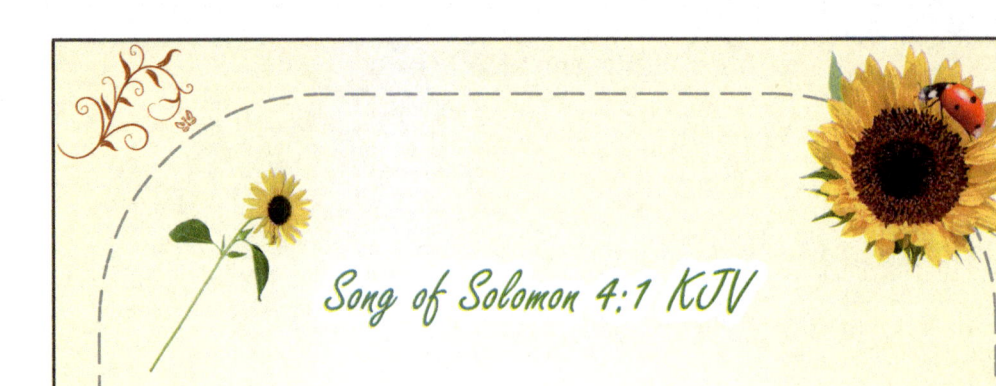

Behold,
  thou art fair,
    my love;

behold,
  thou art fair;
    thou hast doves' eyes
      within thy locks:

thy hair is as a flock of goats,
  that appear from mount Gilead.

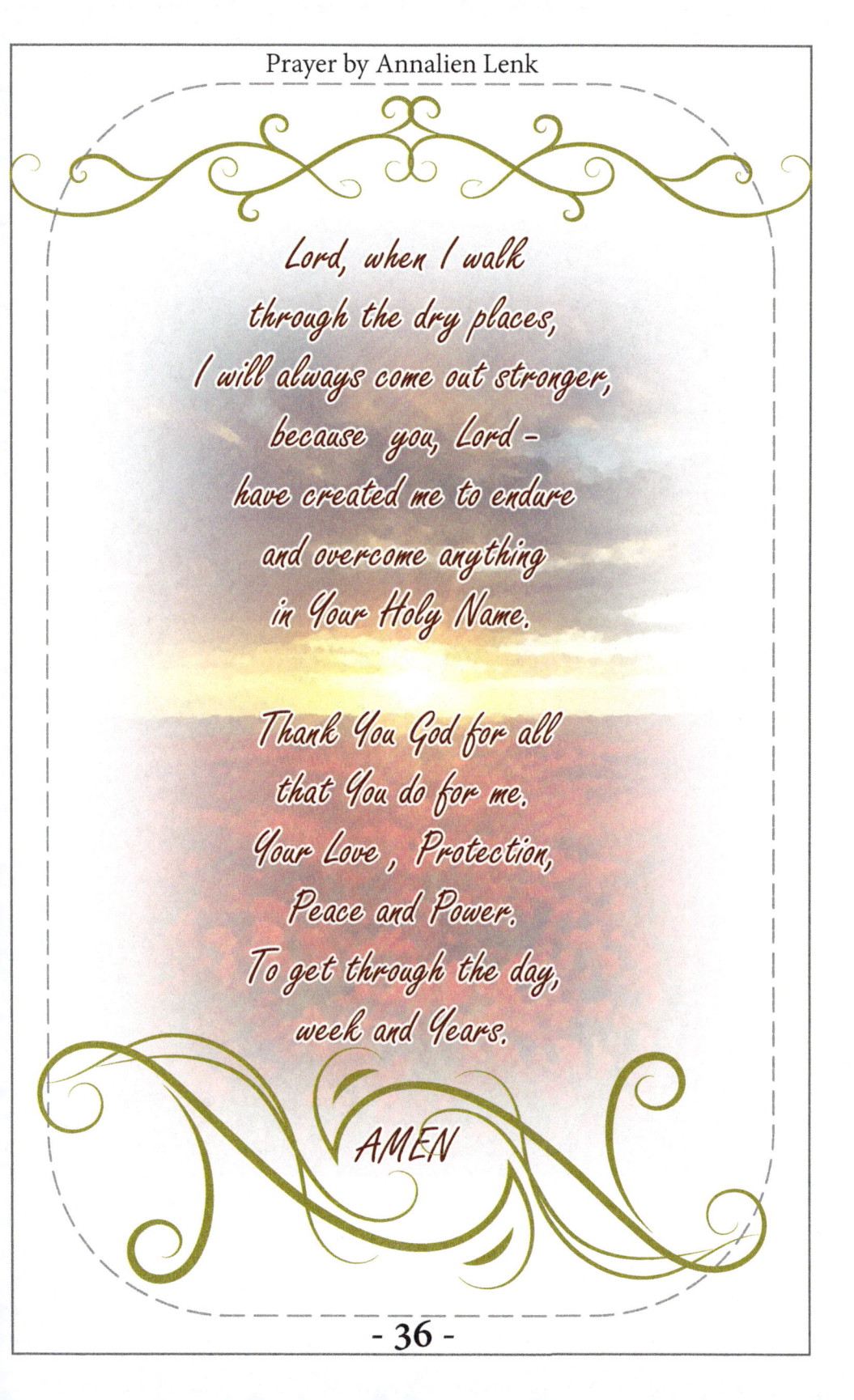

Prayer by Annalien Lenk

Lord, when I walk
through the dry places,
I will always come out stronger,
because you, Lord -
have created me to endure
and overcome anything
in Your Holy Name.

Thank You God for all
that You do for me.
Your Love, Protection,
Peace and Power.
To get through the day,
week and Years.

AMEN

Acts 18:24-26 KJV

And a certain Jew named Apollos, born at Alexandria, an eloquent man, and mighty in the scriptures, came to Ephesus.

This man was instructed in the way of the Lord; and being fervent in the spirit, he spoke and taught diligently the things of the Lord, knowing only the baptism of John.

And he began to speak boldly in the synagogue: whom when Aquila and Priscilla had heard, they took him unto them, and expounded unto him the way of God more perfectly.

Prayer by Annalien Lenk

Dear Lord,
please give me strength today,
for facing my troubles and trails.

Let me see my blessings
and give me courage
to walk in the path
that you have set out for me.

Guide my thoughts
so that I can walk with gratitude
in my heart.

AMEN

Deuteronomy 22:5 KJV

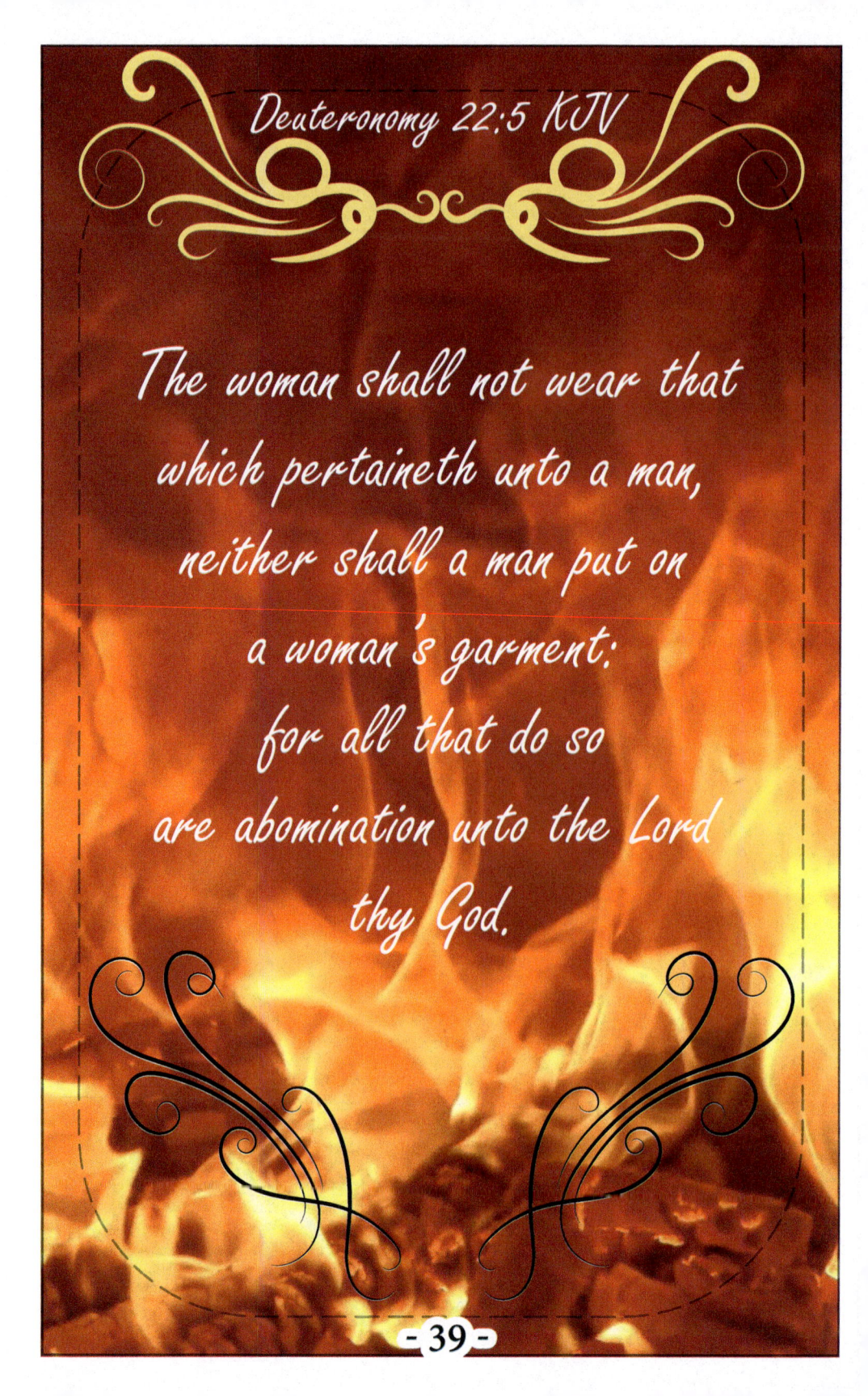

The woman shall not wear that which pertaineth unto a man, neither shall a man put on a woman's garment: for all that do so are abomination unto the Lord thy God.

Prayer by Annalien Lenk

Lord I pray
as a virtuous women
who has accepted
Jesus as my Lord
and Saviour,
to always submit
to Your authority.

I am Your child
and will be righteously clothed.

I submit to my husband
as the Bible commands,
for my husband
has authority over me
and God has authority over him.

I will not compete for authority,
leadership or rulership.

Love You Father.

AMEN

Romans 16:1-2 KJV

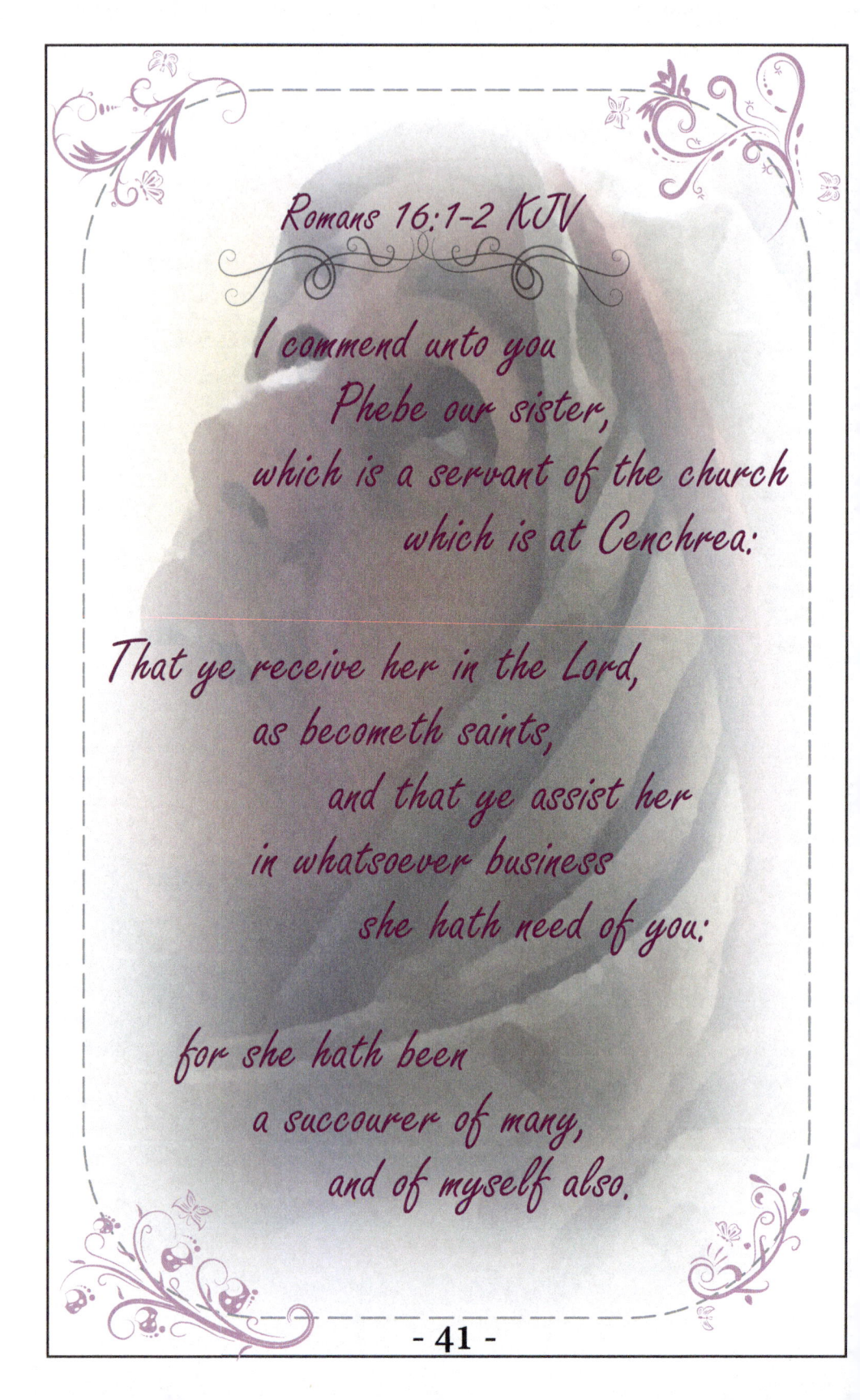

I commend unto you
Phebe our sister,
which is a servant of the church
which is at Cenchrea:

That ye receive her in the Lord,
as becometh saints,
and that ye assist her
in whatsoever business
she hath need of you:

for she hath been
a succourer of many,
and of myself also.

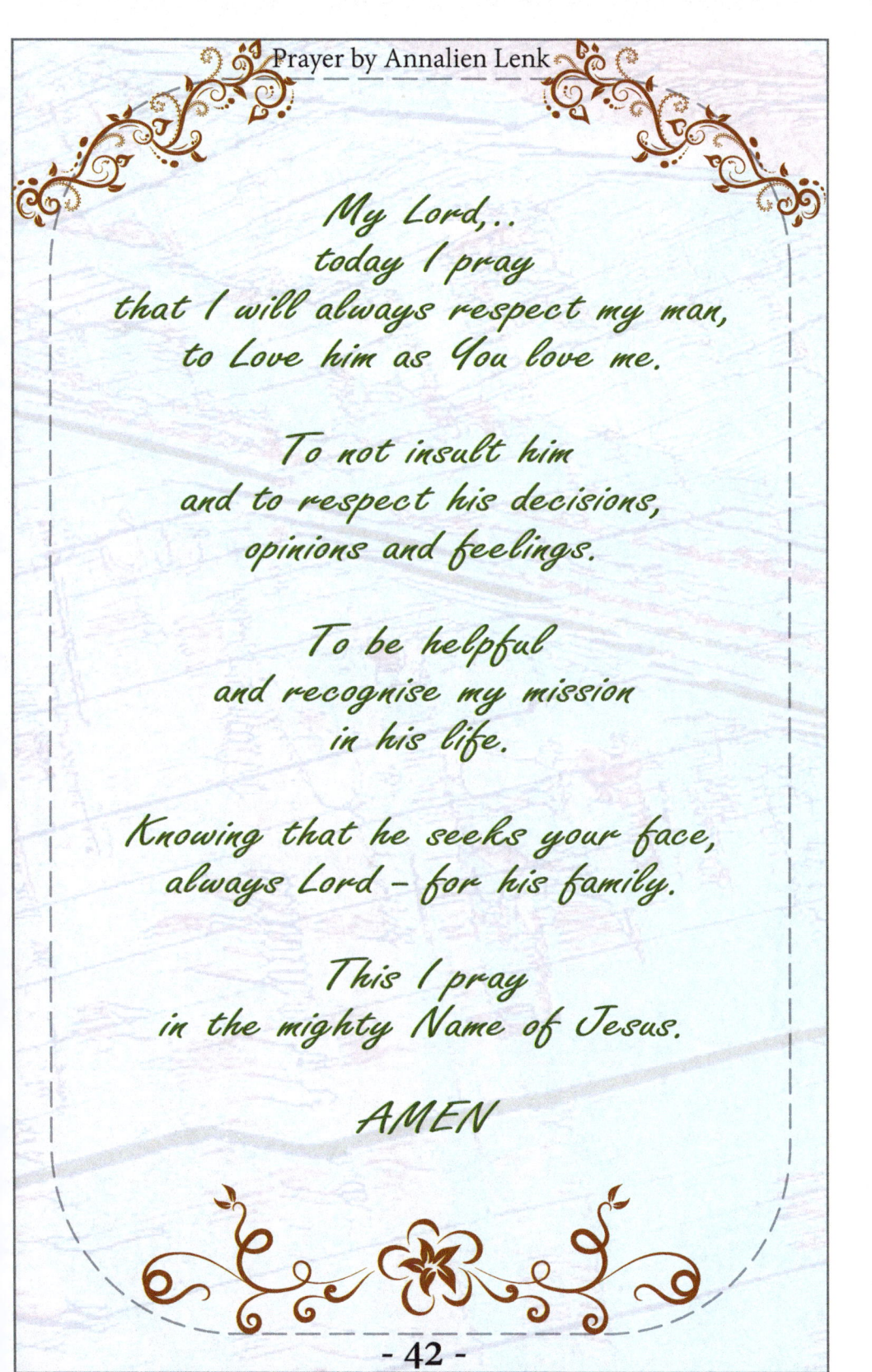

Prayer by Annalien Lenk

My Lord,..
today I pray
that I will always respect my man,
to Love him as You love me.

To not insult him
and to respect his decisions,
opinions and feelings.

To be helpful
and recognise my mission
in his life.

Knowing that he seeks your face,
always Lord – for his family.

This I pray
in the mighty Name of Jesus.

AMEN

Titus 2:1 KJV

But speak thou the things which become sound doctrine:

Prayer by Annalien Lenk

God,
may I not only be
a consumer
but a contributor, too.

To support my family spirituality,
as also intellectually..
And may lovingkindness
be always on my face,
no matter what
I am going through.

AMEN

John 3:16-17 KJV

For God so loved the world,
that he gave his only begotten Son,
that whosoever believeth in Him
should not perish, but have everlasting life.

For God sent not his Son into the world
to condemn the world;
but that the world through him might be saved.

Prayer by Annalien Lenk

Lord mould me
    to always be a woman
      of a deeper love..
        ..a deeper level of love.

A pure love for others.

      A beautifully inward
        and outward love,
that shows your character, Lord.

Just like you did
hanging on that cross for us.

May I always be humble
    until I see you my Lord.

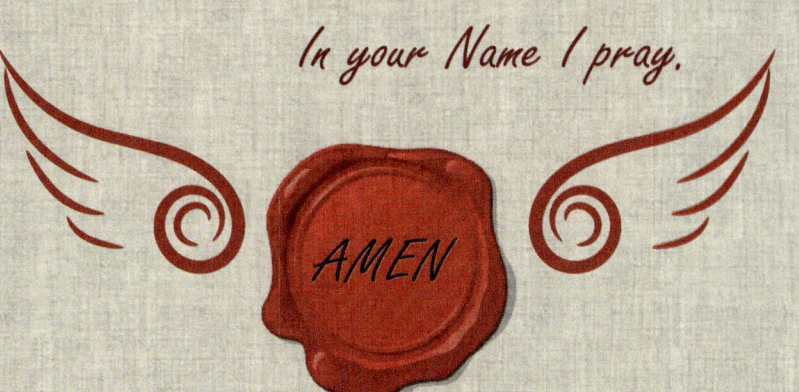

      In your Name I pray.

AMEN

Psalm 28:7 KJV

*The Lord is my strength
and my shield;
my heart trusted in him,
and I am helped;*

*therefore my heart greatly rejoiceth;
and with my song will I praise him.*

Prayer by Millie Smith

To my father in heaven..

Lord, thank you
for being strength
and shield
in times of trouble.

Teach me to let go
and be still
when a storm comes my way,
because I know
where my help comes from
as I sit under the shadow
of your wings.

In Jesus name,

Amen

Psalm 23:2-6 KJV

He maketh me to lie down in green pastures:
He leadeth me beside the still waters.
He restoreth my soul:
He leadeth me in the paths of righteousness
for his name's sake.

Yea, though I walk through the valley
of the shadow of death,
I will fear no evil: for thou art with me;
Thy rod and thy staff they comfort me.

Thou preparest a table before me
in the presence of mine enemies:
Thou anointest my head with oil;
my cup runneth over.

Surely goodness and mercy
shall follow me all the days of my life:
And I will dwell in the house of the LORD
for ever.

Prayer by Millie Smith

Dear Father in heaven,
 thank you for your guidance
 and care in all my days.

You alone are my resting place
 and thank you for always
  keeping me safe, loved and comforted.

My Lord, you are my Shepherd
 and you are all I need right now.

Continue to protect me
 and my loved ones.

May I listen to your voice
 in the places you are guiding me.

Because I know you are
 the ultimate promise keeper
 and way maker.

In your previous name I pray.

Amen

Proverbs 14:1 KJV

Every wise woman buildeth her house:

but the foolish plucketh it down with her hands.

Prayer by Millie Smith

Father God,
 help me to build a firm foundation
  for my life and family.

That I will be deeply rooted
 in your word and the relationship
  I have with you,

so that when a storm comes
 I will not fall.

In Jesus name I pray.

Amen

Psalm 139:14 KJV

*I will praise thee;
for I am fearfully
and wonderfully made:*

*marvellous are thy works;
and that my soul
knoweth right well.*

Prayer by Millie Smith

O'Lord,

    help me to see
        how you see me
    for I am made in your image.

        Lord, you are the potter
        and I am the clay
        because I am uniquely
        and wonderfully made
        with your breath of life
        flowing within me.

Amen and Amen.

Proverbs 31:16-17 KJV

*She considereth a field,
and buyeth it:
with the fruit of her hands
she planteth a vineyard.*

*She girdeth her loins
with strength,
and strengtheneth her arms.*

Prayer by Millie Smith

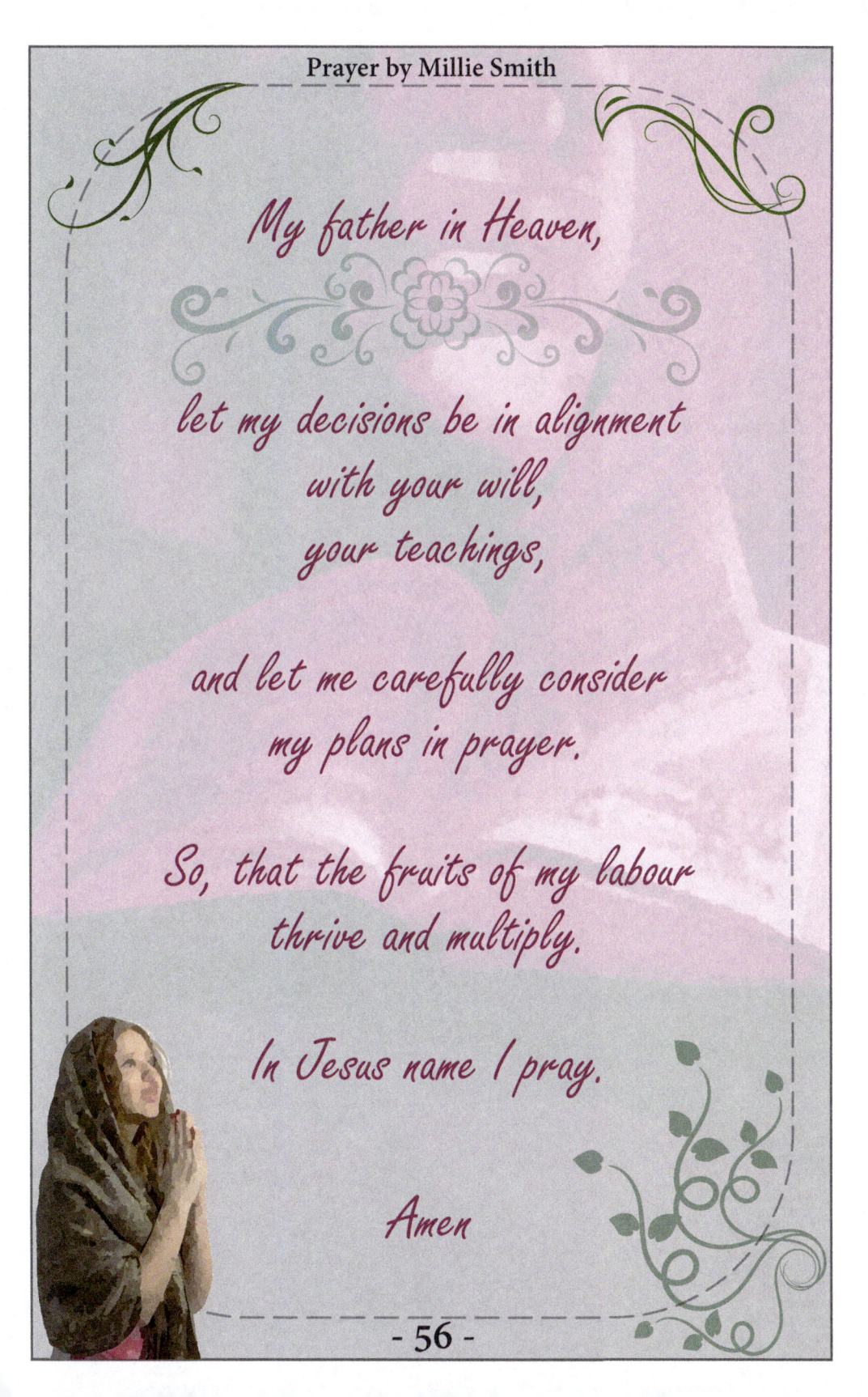

My father in Heaven,

*let my decisions be in alignment
with your will,
your teachings,*

*and let me carefully consider
my plans in prayer.*

*So, that the fruits of my labour
thrive and multiply.*

In Jesus name I pray.

Amen

1 Peter 2:13-17 KJV

Submit yourselves
 to every ordinance of man
  for the Lord's sake:

   whether it be to the king,
    as supreme; Or unto governors,
     as unto them that are sent by him
      for the punishment of evildoers,
       and for the praise of them that do well.

For so is the will of God,
 that with well doing
  ye may put to silence
 the ignorance of foolish men:

   As free, and not using your liberty
    for a cloke of maliciousness,
     but as the servants of God.

Honour all men. Love the brotherhood.

      Fear God.

Prayer by Annalien Lenk

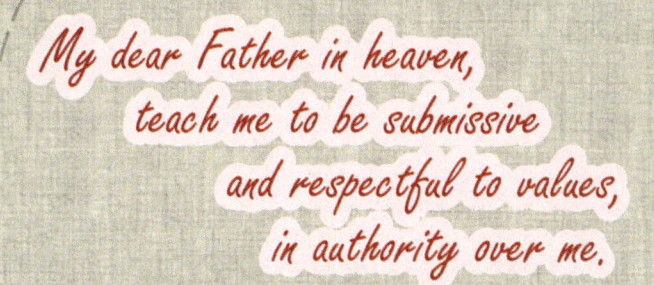

My dear Father in heaven,
teach me to be submissive
and respectful to values,
in authority over me.

Help me be a Light
in our dark world.

Let You Lord, my God,
shine through me always
so that I could be a servant
to you forever.

This I ask
in the wonderful name
of my lord and saviour,
Jesus Christ.

Amen

Acts 1:12-14 KJV

Then returned they unto Jerusalem
from the mount called Olivet,
which is from Jerusalem a sabbath day's journey.

And when they were come in,
they went up into an upper room,
where abode both Peter, and James,
and John, and Andrew, Philip,
and Thomas, Bartholomew, and Matthew,
James the son of Alphaeus,
and Simon Zelotes,
and Judas the brother of James.

These all continued with one accord
in prayer and supplication,
with the women, and Mary the mother of Jesus,
and with his brethren.

Prayer by Annalien Lenk

My dear Heavenly Father,
today I pray
to have unstoppable joy,

because of Your Amazing Grace
that you reached down..

May I always be in one accord
with You my Lord
and never lean on my own understanding.

May I live with Joy and Peace
in my live, each and every day.

I thank you Lord
for all the goodness
that you have ever bestowed upon me.

In the name of the Father, the Son
and the Holy Spirit.

Amen

Luke 23:49 KJV

And all his acquaintance, and the women that followed him from Galilee,

stood afar off, beholding these things.

Prayer by Annalien Lenk

*My Lord,
today I pray for mercy on my soul.*

*I pray that Your grace and strength
will always be with me,
for You God – has called me
to walk in the light.*

*Look inside of my heart,
so that Your life can shine
right through me,*

*so that others can see
what I carry inside.*

*I will always be
a shining light for you,
my God.*

*This I pray
in Your wonderful name.*

AMEN

1 Peter 3:4 KJV

But let it be
 the hidden man
  of the heart,
   in that which
      is not corruptible,
    even the ornament
  of a meek and quiet spirit,
 which is in the sight of God
of great price.

Prayer by Annalien Lenk

Oh Lord, today I pray
that I might be the Spotless Bride
that You have been waiting for –
me to be.

To be pure
and to always trust
in your word, my Lord.

Even in my quietness, Lord
I will always obey-
and love You,
with all my heart.

For You, Lord,
have paid the greatest price
for my life,
I will forever be in Your presence.

This I pray in Your holy, mighty
and wonderful name..

..my King of Kings,
my Lord of Lords,
my beginning and my end.

Amen.

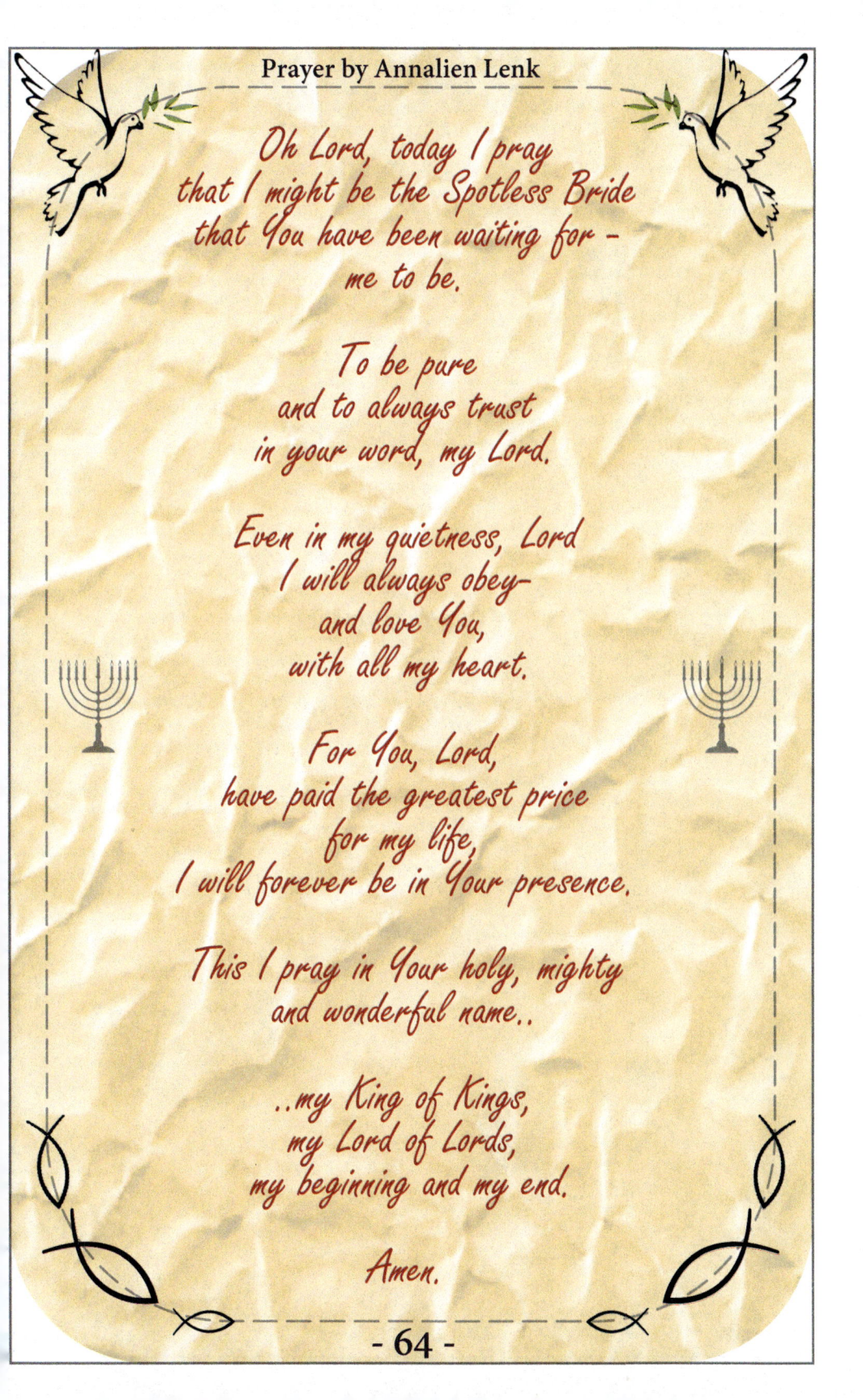

Colossians 3:19 KJV

Husbands, love your wives, and be not bitter against them.

Prayer by Annalien Lenk

Dear Father in heaven,
today I pray for my husband,
that he would love me forever..
and he would always remember our vows.

That he would never
get bitter thoughts against me,
always talk
and sort disagreements out
between us.

For what you have joined together,
let no man come between.

I pray that he will always stay
in your word and love you,
just as much as I do.

I pray that he would
always treat me,
like you treat the church.

I love You Lord
and always will.

In Your Name I pray.

Amen

Genesis 21:12 KJV

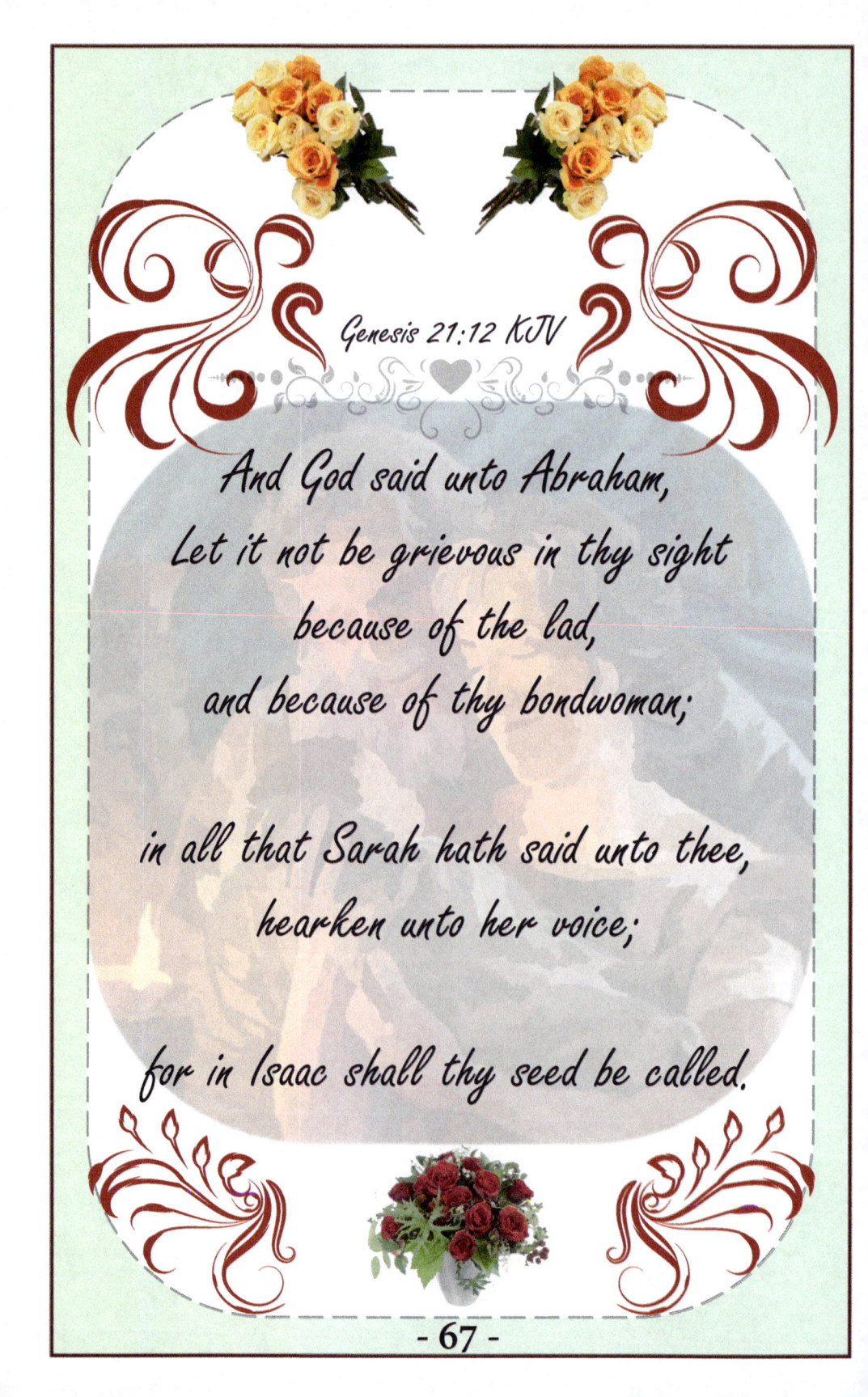

And God said unto Abraham,
Let it not be grievous in thy sight
because of the lad,
and because of thy bondwoman;

in all that Sarah hath said unto thee,
hearken unto her voice;

for in Isaac shall thy seed be called.

Prayer by Annalien Lenk

My dear Holy Lord in heaven,
be merciful to me oh Lord
when I reach out to you
day and night..

Lord I open my heart,
my soul and my mind to You.

With all of my burdens,
I give them over to You.

Full me with joy, Lord.

You are so good,
so ready to forgive,
so full of unfailing love..

All I ask for is help.

You always listen
to my prayers, Lord.

I asked today,
that You will
always keep me close to you
and listen
to all my prayers.

In my Father's Name I pray.

Amen

1 Corinthians 11:3-10 KJV

But I would have you know
that the head of every man is Christ;
and the head of the woman is the man;
and the head of Christ is God.

Every man praying or prophesying,
having his head covered,
dishonoureth his head.

But every woman that prayeth
or prophesieth with her head uncovered
dishonoureth her head:
for that is even all one
as if she were shaven.

For if the woman be not covered,
let her also be shorn:
but if it be a shame for a woman
to be shorn or shaven,
let her be covered.

For a man indeed ought not to cover his head,
forasmuch as he is the image and glory of God:
but the woman is the glory of the man.

For the man is not of the woman:
but the woman of the man.

Neither was the man created for the woman;
but the woman for the man.

For this cause ought the woman
to have power on...

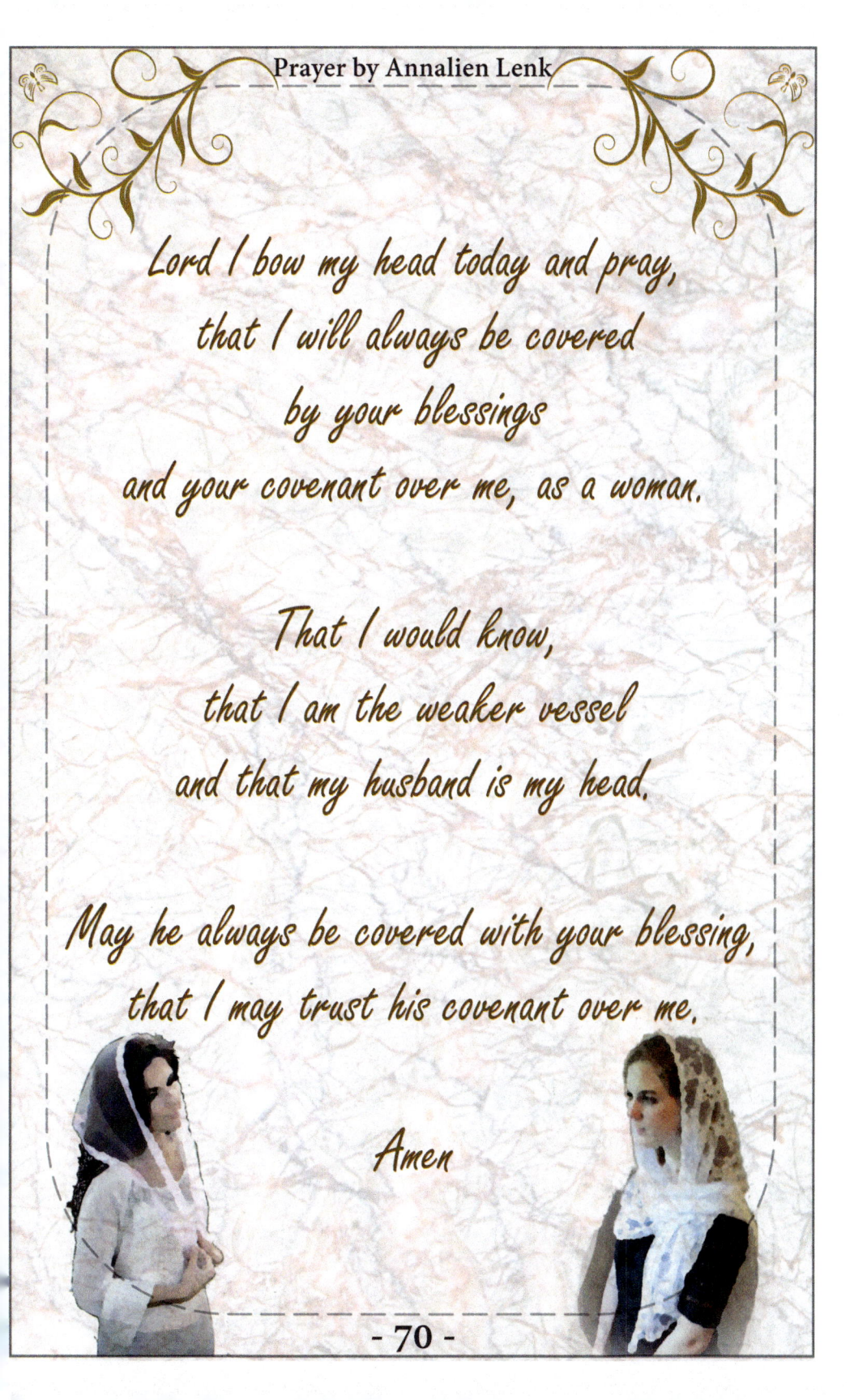

Prayer by Annalien Lenk

Lord I bow my head today and pray,
that I will always be covered
by your blessings
and your covenant over me, as a woman.

That I would know,
that I am the weaker vessel
and that my husband is my head.

May he always be covered with your blessing,
that I may trust his covenant over me.

Amen

Mark 15:40-41 KJV

There were also women
looking on afar off:
among whom
was Mary Magdalene,
and Mary
the mother of James the less
and of Joses, and Salome;
(Who also, when he was in Galilee,
followed him, and ministered unto him;)
and many other women
which came up
with him unto Jerusalem.

Prayer by Annalien Lenk

*Oh my Lord, God in Heaven,
I Love You So much.*

*My Loving Heavenly Father
I thank You for Your Amazing Love
and Grace.*

*Save me from eternal separation
from You Lord.
I humbly thank You
that You became sin on my behalf.*

*I want to always stand
in Awe of you, Lord.*

Forever and Ever.

This I pray, today..

Amen

Ephesians 4:24 KJV

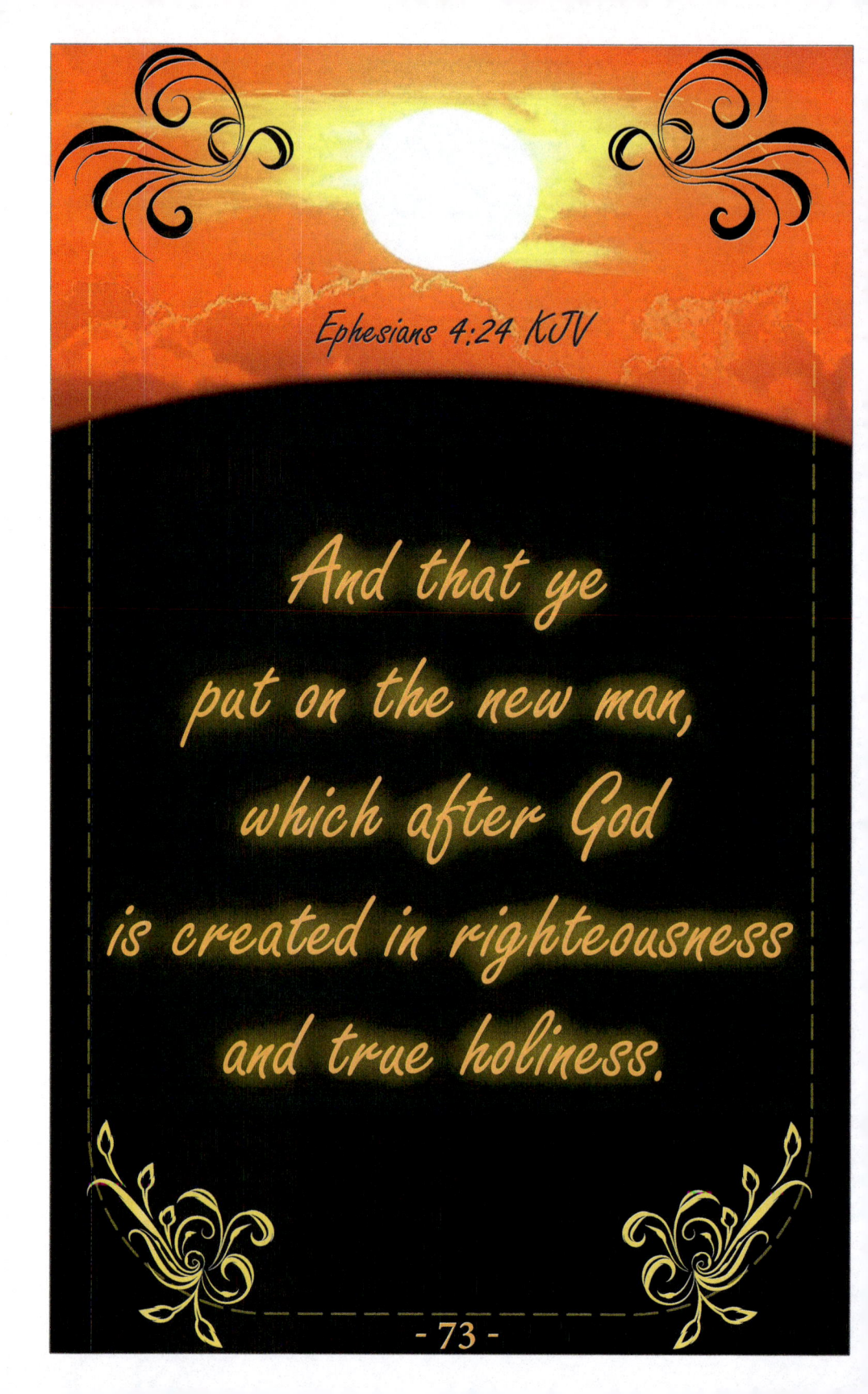

And that ye
put on the new man,
which after God
is created in righteousness
and true holiness.

Prayer by Annalien Lenk

*My dear Lord,
my righteous and Holy Father...*

*I pray
that I can completely
put the old me away,
my old nature, my worldly life
and all my wrong doings.*

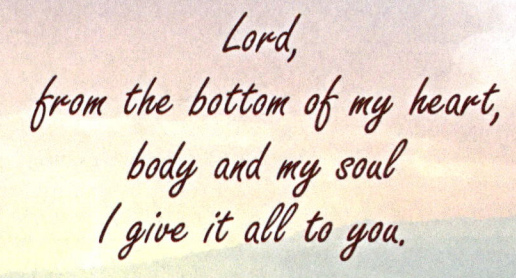

*Lord,
from the bottom of my heart,
body and my soul
I give it all to you.*

*My life is yours,
oh precious Father..*

My thoughts are yours, Father.

All the glory goes to You, Lord.

Amen

Psalm 139:13-16 KJV

For thou hast possessed my reins:
thou hast covered me in my mother's womb.
I will praise thee;
for I am fearfully and wonderfully made:
marvellous are thy works;
and that my soul knoweth right well.

My substance was not hid from thee,
when I was made in secret,
and curiously wrought
in the lowest parts of the earth.

Thine eyes did see my substance,
yet being unperfect;
and in thy book
all my members were written,
which in continuance were fashioned,
when as yet there was none of them.

Prayer by Annalien Lenk

My God,
I adore Thee,
what a Joy it is to know
that You know me Lord.

You know all my happiness, Joy
and also know every tear
that I shed.

You know my pain, my heart break
and my long-suffering.

You know everything about me.

I will always praise
and worship you,
for I am made fearfully
and wonderfully by you.

I will never let You down, intentionally.

With Your help and guidance
I will live,
until I see You in Heaven.

Amen

Printed in Great Britain
by Amazon